The Illustrated War Reports

Ypres 1914-1915

Contemporary Combat Images from the Great War

First published in this format in Great Britain in 2015 by
Pen & Sword Military
An imprint of
Pen & Sword Books Ltd
47 Church Street
Barnsley
South Yorkshire
S70 2AS

ISBN 978 1 47383 788 1

A CIP catalogue record for this book is available from the British Library.

Printed and bound in Malta
By Gutenberg Press Ltd.

Pen & Sword Books Ltd incorporates the Imprints of Aviation, Atlas, Family History, Fiction, Maritime, Military, Discovery, Politics, History, Archaeology, Select, Wharncliffe Local History, Wharncliffe True Crime, Military Classics, Wharncliffe Transport, Leo Cooper, The Praetorian Press, Remember When, Seaforth Publishing and Frontline Publishing.

For a complete list of Pen & Sword titles please contact
PEN & SWORD BOOKS LIMITED
47 Church Street, Barnsley, South Yorkshire, S70 2AS, England
E-mail: enquiries@pen-and-sword.co.uk
Website: www.pen-and-sword.co.uk

Contents

An introduction to the series

The photographic equipment in use during the Great War was cumbersome and bulky and the environment of the trenches was highly lethal. As a result, the ability to take snapshots was extremely limited, making it all but impossible to capture meaningful shots of the fleeting moments of action. Furthermore the output of cameramen was subject to intense censorship; in consequence, action sequences from the front were so rare and sanitised that the popular magazines reporting the events, on both sides of the line, were forced to recruit artists and illustrators to fill the gap.

These artists were called upon to produce a highly accurate visual record of the events the camera could not capture; hand to hand fighting, trench raids, aerial dogfights, sea battles, desperate last stands, individual acts of heroism, night actions and cavalry charges. They were there to record events on the battlefield for commercial purposes and their work usually found a home in popular magazines such as 'The War Illustrated'; the result of their efforts was a huge body of work which spanned the full gamut of styles ranging from the simplest of sketches through to highly finished oil paintings on a grand scale.

In their foremost ranks were skilled technicians such as Richard Caton-Woodville Jr. and William Barnes Wollen both of whom can stand comparison with the great artists of any age. Many of these artists including, of course, Richard Caton-Woodville Jr. had served in the military. They were amazingly talented and their work is of superb quality. They also had the eye for detail in terms of uniform, equipment and weapons which brings added authenticity to their work. They were also able to conjure up for the viewer an impression of the genuine stresses and strains of combat from the soldier's point of view.

The Second Battle of Ypres by Barnes Wollen

The canon of works by these two great artists alone includes such masterpieces as Barnes Wollen's Landrecies, 25 August 1914, The Defeat of the Prussian Guard, Ypres, 1914, The Canadians at Ypres and The London Territorials at Poziers. Richard Caton-Woodville Jr.'s works include The Piper of Loos, The Battle of the Somme, The 2nd Batt. Manchester Regiment taking Six Guns at dawn near St. Quentin, The Entry of the 5th Lancers into Mons, The Charge of the 9th Lancers at Moncel, 7 September 1914, and the magnificent Halloween, 1914: Stand of the London Scottish on Messines Ridge.

The charge of the 9th Lancers at a German battery near Mons by Richard Caton Woodville Jr.

It is a strange state of affairs but even with such luminaries to call upon, the work of the contemporary combat illustrators of the Great War, for illustrative purposes, is today almost entirely overlooked in favour of the work of the photographers.

The reason for this sad state of affairs lies in the fact that, besides the excellent work by the likes of the brilliant Barnes Wollen, there was an army of more pedestrian artists at work and many of the lesser gifted were engaged in turning out crude images to feed the populist pages of the consumer publishing machine. Primarily as a result of their efforts the whole corpus of wartime illustration has become tainted with the tag of propaganda, and in consequence the remarkable work of even the greatest of Great War graphic artists is now extremely unfashionable. It is considered to be vulgar and is routinely dismissed as melodramatic and jingoistic and all too often mischaracterised simply as crude populist propaganda. Publishers now turn their backs on these works which are no longer considered worthy to illustrate modern history books.

Things That Matter. Colonel Fitz-Shrapnel receives the following message from "G.H.Q." "Please let us know, as soon as possible, the number of tins of raspberry jam issued to you last Friday"

Another group at work in the trenches were the humorists and chief among those was the peerless Bruce Bairnsfather. Bairnsfather had seen action during 1914 and 1915 as a

The Kensingtons at Laventie by Eric Kennington

machine gun officer serving with the Warwickshire Regiment. His finely observed work grew out of his experience in the Ypres salient and began to appear in The Bystander during 1915. By 1917 Bairnsfather was already one of the most widely recognised artist/illustrators of his day, but in our day his work is viewed as holding little relevance for serious students of the Great War. This is a great shame as his finely crafted observations have a great deal to tell us concerning the appalling conditions endured with such stoicism by the British troops on the Ypres salient serving under the shadow of the German trenches.

Fortunately there remains a wider appreciation for the work of the official war artists. We can be thankful that, in addition to the work of the still photographers and the illustrators, there was a general appreciation by the governments of all sides that, as well as the simple act of recording the events, there was also the need to record that which "the camera cannot interpret".

The British government in particular came to the gradual realisation that "a war so epic in its scope by land, sea and air, and so detailed and complex in its mechanism", required interpretation, not just by technicians, but also by artists and this led to the appointment of the first official war artists. The War Artists were able to present a vivid picture of the world as it really was, in full colour, just like our own world and today, through their work we are privileged to have access to a remarkable record of tho Great War which brings back the dimension of colour to an otherwise grey world.

The British official war artists were a select group of artists who were employed on contract, or commissioned to produce specific works during the Great War. However it wasn't until May 1916, some two years after the outbreak of the war, that the British Government appointed Muirhead Bone as Britain's first official war artist.

Ready to start by William Orpen

Official war artists were appointed by governments to record events as a matter of record but others were commissioned for propaganda purposes. War artists depicted diverse aspects of the Great War through his or her art; this might be a pictorial record or a comment on some other aspect of war or it might seek to cast a light on how war blights lives. Muirhead Bone worked exclusively in pencil and ink with publication in Government magazines in mind. As a result, through his work, we still see the world in the same monochrome shades as the official photographs.

However, after Bone returned to England, he was replaced by his brother-in-law Francis Dodd. It is disappointing that Dodd specialised mainly in portraits many of which could just as easily have been created at home. They throw little light on the nature of the Great War. In addition Dodd was very sparing in his use of colour, but the muted red shades which occasionally creep into his work indicated that the door to the world of colour was at last sliding open. Mercifully, in 1917, arrangements were made to send other artists who possessed greater artistic ambition to France. Included in their ranks was Eric Kennington who is best known for his painting of 'The Kensingtons at Laventie' which depicted his former unit at rest during a lull in the hard-fought battles of 1915. Although there were no official war artists before 1916, Kennington had already served at the front with the 13th Battalion of The London Regiment who were known as 'The Kensingtons', he saw action from 1914 until he was invalided out in June 1915 after accidentally shooting himself in the toe!

The famous painting was constructed from memory and depicts the artist in 1915 standing behind and to the right of the soldier in the white hat. Kennington recreates the scene as his platoon rested in a village after four sleepless days and nights in the snow covered trenches. The exhausted men are waiting for the order to march on to

1st Artist Rifles by Paul Nash

a warm billet and the picture conveys that sense of almost dreamlike weariness. With Kennington we at last begin to experience the world of the Great War, not as a hum-drum monochrome but as a world of emotion and colour. It was also the beginning of a trend which was to lead to a remarkable body of work as artists on both sides worked to capture the essence of the events as they saw them.

William Orpen was another official war painter who was able to open a door to the events of the Great War. In 1917 he travelled to the Western Front and along with the usual official portraits of generals and politicians he produced drawings and paintings of private soldiers, dead soldiers and German prisoners of war. His self portrait ' Ready To Start' depicts the artist reflected in a mirror while preparing to set off for duty in the Front Line and neatly encapsulates the manner on which war intrudes on the ordinary world.

For his war work, Orpen was made a Knight Commander of the Order of the British Empire. He was selected as a member of the Royal Academy in 1919. Orpen gave most of his war time works, some 138 in all, to the British government on the understanding that they should be framed in simple white frames and kept together as a single body of work. They are now in the collection of the Imperial War Museum in London. William Orpen came to loathe the politicians who prolonged the Great War but he also relied upon them for post-war commissions so he chose to embody his subtle criticism in his work.

Orpen produced some very strong work during the war, but interestingly he was also present at the political wrangling after the war. His large paintings of the Versailles Peace Conference feature a rather insolent focus on the gilt trappings of the room rather than the politicians gathered there. There is an emphasis on distortion. By doing that he made a strong statement concerning the distorted nature of the political wranglings and the insignificance of the politicians compared to framework which was built on the sufferings of those who made the golden prospects of peace possible.

Even more outspoken was the artist who, like Orpen, witnessed the events in France, he was Paul Nash. The young Paul Nash reluctantly enlisted in the Artists' Rifles and was sent to the Western Front in February 1917 by which time he was a second lieutenant in the Hampshire Regiment. A few days before the Third Ypres offensive he fell into a trench, broke a rib and was invalided home. While recuperating in London, Nash worked from his front-line sketches to produce a series of works which accentuated the harshness of the war. His work such as the celebrated paintings Over The Top (the 1st Artist Rifles at Marcoing), the Menin Road and the Ypres Salient at Night embodies the influence of the Vorticist movement, in fact it became the vanguard of that movement and was well received when it was exhibited later that year at the Goupil Gallery. His work was also featured in 'Blast' magazine.

The staff of the Propaganda Bureau were naturally wary of the anti-war sympathies which were embodied in the work of Paul Nash and they subjected the artist to particularly strict control. Nash objected to such censorship and he recorded his views in a letter home to his wife dated 16th November 1916 in which he wrote, "I am no longer an artist interested and curious, I am a messenger who will bring back word from the men who are fighting to those who want the war to go on for ever. Feeble, inarticulate, will be my message, but it will have a bitter truth, and may it burn their lousy souls."

The story of the men who fought in the Great War was tough and brutal, but even worse was the experience of those who were maimed by shellfire or poisoned by gas. The artist who was best positioned to highlight their plight was Christopher R. W. Nevinson.

At the outbreak of the war Nevinson joined the Friends' Ambulance Unit, which his father had helped to found, and was deeply disturbed by his work tending wounded French soldiers. For a brief period he served as a volunteer ambulanceman, in 1915, ill health forced his return to Britain.

Nevinson used these experiences as the subject matter for a series of powerful paintings which used Futurist techniques to great effect. His 1916 painting of French Troops Resting is a perfect example of how the modernist style could be harnessed to capture the misery of even day to day life in the war; Nevinson's painting 'La Mitrailleuse' tells us everything we need to know about the industrial nature of the war and Walter Sickert wrote 'this will probably remain the most authoritative and concentrated utterance on the war in the history of painting'.

Nevinson volunteered for home service with the Royal Army Medical Corps, before being invalided out; he was eventually appointed as an official war artist, though his later paintings, based on a short visit to the Western Front, lacked the same powerful reception as those earlier works which had helped to make him one of the most famous young artists working in England. The reason for the loss of impact lies in the fact that, by 1917, Nevinson was no longer finding Modernist styles adequate for describing the horrors of modern war and he switched to a realistic style. Paths of Glory depicts

Gassed by John Singer Sargeant

two fallen British soldiers in a never ending landscape of mud and barbed wire, this particular study is typical of his later war paintings. It is starkly realistic and it's notable for the complete lack of Futurist or Vorticist effects. Similarly, 'A Taube' reflects the human cost of an air raid. We expect to see a Taube, which was a German aircraft, but by juxtaposing the name of the aircraft with the pathetic, lifeless body of a child, Nevinson achieves a far greater effect.

The Great War was fought not just on land, but at sea and in the air. Every bit as important as all of these theatres was the home front where superhuman efforts were required to keep the armed forces in weapons, rations and ammunition. These were the sinews of war and John Lavery was the artist who was recruited to paint pictures of the home front. In this industrial war, what happened at home was every bit as important as the events on the fighting fronts. Without arms, ammunition and the whole paraphernalia that an army needs, everything just grinds to a halt. The labour shortage transformed society by bringing women into the war effort and he did a wonderful job of depicting the effects of the war on the home front. However, we should not overlook the contribution of other outstanding artists working in the same field such as Walter Bayes

who painted the famous image of families taking shelter in the underground.

It's here on the home front that we see female artists at work and artists such as Anna Airy and Flora Lion did a remarkable job of capturing those images of women at work in what had previously been a man's world. The fact that women were not just doing the work but also making the art was a double departure from the norm.

A war artist essentially creates a visual account of war by showing its impact as men and women are shown waiting, preparing, fighting, working, suffering and celebrating. The works produced by war artists are immensely varied and they form an all too often overlooked record of many aspects of war. They record differing aspects of individuals' experience of war, whether allied or enemy, service or civilian, military or political, social or cultural.

Perhaps the most famous painting to emerge from the Great War is Gassed by John Singer Sargeant, it depicts the aftermath of a mustard gas attack on the Western Front in August 1918. In the painting, a line of British soldiers who have been exposed to a gas attack are being led along a duckboard walkway at le Bac-du-sud dressing station by a medical orderly. Their eyes are bandaged as a result of exposure to gas and each man holds on to the shoulder of the man in front. There is another line of temporarily

For What? by Frederick Varley

blinded soldiers in the background, and the artist spares the viewer none of the horrors of war as one soldier is leaning over vomiting onto the ground. In contrast to the agony of suffering in the foreground we see a glimpse into the world of those unaffected by the gas as a football match continues in the background, the players oblivious to the horrors of the foreground scene.

Frederick Varley is one of the most justifiably celebrated war artists and his painting entitled 'For What?', captures the desolate futility of the Great War. His study of captured German prisoners is also exceptional. He seems to be saying to us 'well where's the martial glory in all this?' All this effort and expenditure to round up a few ragged individuals who look more like beggars trudging through a ravaged landscape on a road to nowhere. Everything in the painting just screams waste, folly and emptiness.

The German war artists and illustrators were equally hard at work. Without their efforts we wouldn't have the German perspective on unique events such as the war from the perspective of the crew of a Zeppelin over London. Despite the prevailing national stereotype of the humourless Teuton, the Germans too had their satirists. They mainly found expression in the long running Bavarian humour magazine Simpiccissimus. The artist who has risen to the highest prominence is, of course, Otto Dix, his 'Stormtroopers Advancing Under Gas', is now one of the most famous images to emerge from the Great War. This work was released as both an etching and an aquatint by Dix in 1924. During this period Dix had begun to specialise in the grim reality of the lingering effects

Stormtroopers Advancing Under Gas by Otto Dix

of the war in Weimar Germany. His images of the war wounded and the decaying moral fabric of German society have a haunting quality which still hits home hard even today. Along with George Grosz, Dix is widely considered one of the most important artists of the Neue Sachlichkeit. When the First World War erupted, Dix enthusiastically volunteered for the German Army. He was assigned to a field artillery regiment in Dresden. In the autumn of 1915 he was assigned as a non-commissioned officer of a machine-gun unit on the Western front and took part in the Battle of the Somme. In November 1917, his unit was transferred to the Eastern front until the end of hostilities with Russia, and in February 1918 he was stationed in Flanders. Back on the western front, he fought in the German Spring Offensive. He earned the Iron Cross (second class) and reached the rank of vizefeldwebel. In August of that year he was wounded in the neck, and shortly after he took pilot training lessons. He was discharged from service in December 1918.

Dix was profoundly affected by the sights of the war, and later described a recurring nightmare in which he crawled through destroyed houses. He represented his traumatic experiences in many subsequent works, including a portfolio of fifty etchings called 'Der Krieg', published in 1924.

As the centenary of the Great War approached, I decided the time had come to undertake a full scale reappraisal not just of the Official War Artists but also of the neglected output of the contemporary combat artists and illustrators of the Great War.

It was soon apparent that far from being mere romantic fantasies these long neglected images are often highly accurate in every detail. Where the artist was present these works form a primary source of war reportage which is every bit as important as the written word. These works are often a valid and highly authentic secondary record based on eyewitness accounts. The artists at work during the Great War were able to work with the writers who had witnessed the events and often fighting men themselves and they worked to produce a fresh visual account of the action which could not be recorded by any other means. These illustrations are important as they form a valid record of the reality of the fighting as viewed through contemporary eyes. Taken together these works actually form a priceless picture of how the reality of the action at the front was conveyed to contemporary audiences at a time when the events of the war were still unfolding.

Bob Carruthers 2014

Chapter 1

The Road To Ypres

The Battle of the Frontiers is the collective name for the series of battles fought along the eastern frontier of France and in southern Belgium shortly after the outbreak of World War I. After two months of bitter fighting the Allies were eventually able to thwart the German Aufmarsch II deployment plan which had been devised by Helmuth von Moltke the Younger but more widely known as the Schlieffen plan. The German concentration on the right (northern) flank, was to wheel through Belgium and attack the French in the rear, but was delayed by the presence of the British Expeditionary Force (BEF) on the left flank of the French armies. On 23 August, the German IX Corps advanced and part of the 35th Brigade got across the Mons–Condé Canal east of Nimy. The British, who were operating east of Mons, were pushed back after a stand on the Mons-Givry road.

The German II Cavalry Corps was to head towards Denain to cut off the British retreat but the BEF avoided the net and the Franco-British were driven back by the Germans, who were able to invade almost all of Belgium and a great slice of northern France. However French and British rearguard actions delayed the German advance, allowing the French time to transfer their forces to the west to defend Paris, resulting in the First Battle of the Marne known to posterity as the miracle on the Marne.

Bringing up the guns - British artillery getting into position at the battle of Mons

Sir Philip Chetwode

General Sir Horace Lockwood Smith-Dorrien G.C.B., D.S.O.

British infantry with the bayonet

The unquenchable cheerfulness of the British soldier

The glorious charge of the Ninth Lancers

Above: British reinforcements brought up by bus
Opposite: German column mowed down by British machine guns at Landrecies

Flashing the signal to charge by searchlight

Hands up method of
German surrender

The battle of Cambrai where the Gordons were trapped by the enemy

W.B. Wollen

War beneath the Earth

Irish fusiliers attack with the bayonet

Aug 25th 1914, Grenadiers and Irish guards fighting from a house

Irish guards at prayer before going into action

British infantry withstanding 9000 Prussian cavalry at Le Cateau Aug 26th 1914

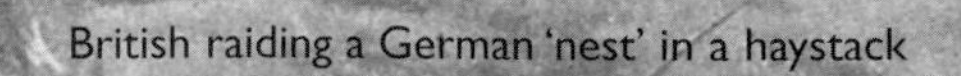

British raiding a German 'nest' in a haystack

How Lance Corporal Jarvis won the VC at Jemappes

An incident in the hard-fought retreat from Belgium - British troops on the river bank prepared to resist the German advance

Bagpipes in the trenches

Scene of the heroic stand of L Battery RHA near Compiegne

Holding a British position on the Mons-Conde canal

British charge at Hooge - where trenches lost through German 'liquid fire' were recaptured

British artillery officer's heroism at Tournal

Huge shells bursting harmlessly in a British trench

British valour near Compiegne. How three gunners of the RHA won a place in history

Battle of the Marne - mixed forces of British and Turks fight the Germans for possession of a village in Brie.

Opening the flood gates at Flanders

British infantry dislodging the Germans

British army service corps running to and fro along trenches delivering bully beef and bread to soldiers

British artillery men working their guns amid a hail of German projectiles

Men of Royal Army Medical corps searching for wounded in a wood at nighttime

Lieutenant General Sir Douglas Haig

Top left: Heroism of the Mudlarks
Above: Death in a barn
Left: British log artillery draws the German fire

British troops resting in a disused quarry on the Aisne

The brain of the army protected from German shells

British burrows in the battle of the Aisne

Northamptons treacherously cut down by an enemy ambush

Opposite: Warlife in a sandpit behind the British lines in the champagne country

An artillery duel in a thunderstorm

Smashing a pontoon bridge across the Morin

The peril of the non-combatant, a thrilling adventure with a Red Cross wagon.

The moment of farewell - A touching scene at Victoria Station during wartime

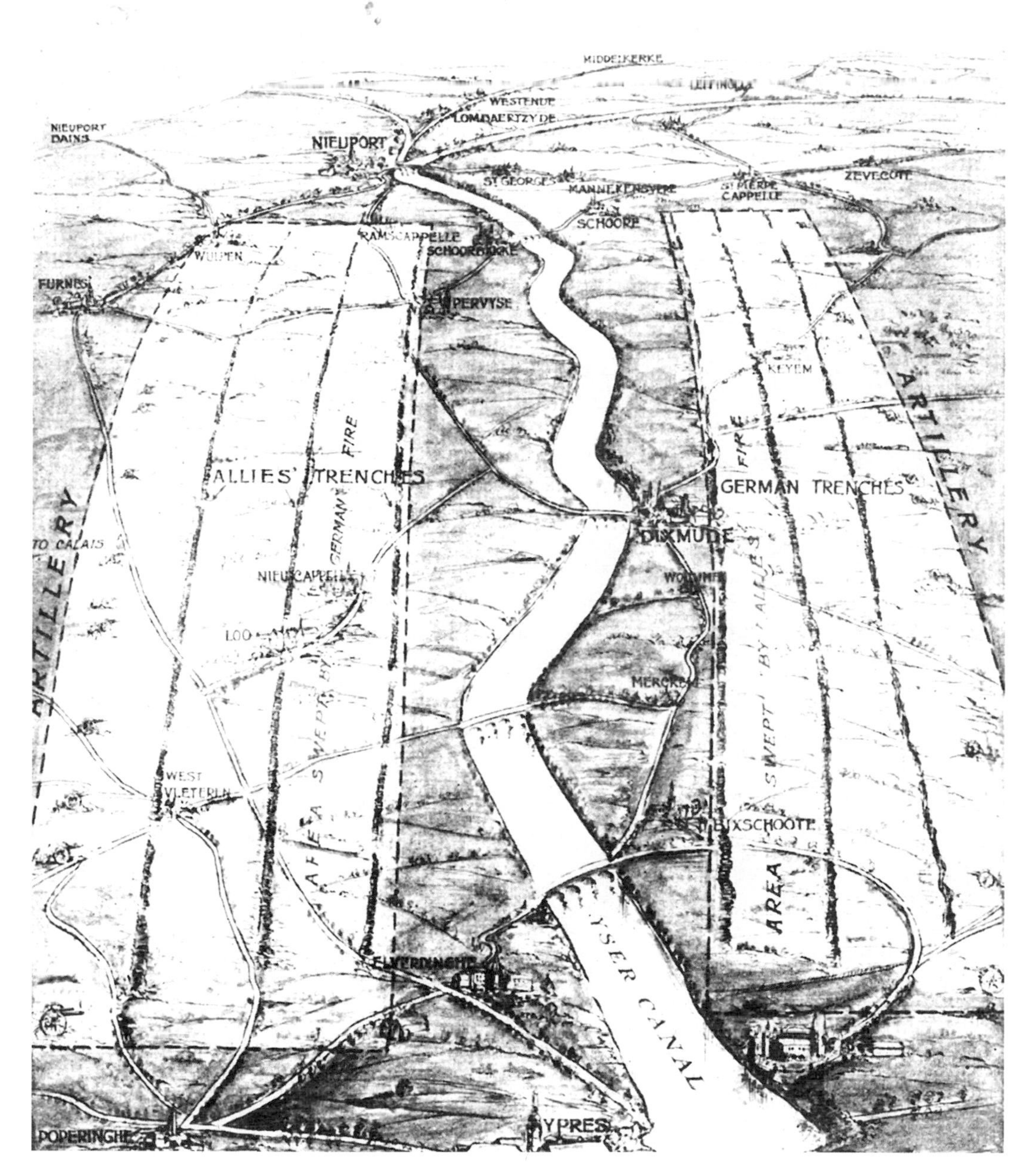

Deadlock along the Yser

Chapter 2

The Salient is Formed

The Ypres Salient was the name given by the British to the area around Ypres in Belgium which was the scene of some of the most titanic struggles of the Great War. The salient was a bulge into the German lines which was formed by British, French, Canadian and Belgian defensive efforts against German incursion during the series of 1914 battles known as "Race to the Sea". These actions culminated in the Battle of the Yser and the First Battle of Ypres. These battles saved the Ypres salient and the corner of Belgium around Veurne from occupation, but also led to the beginning of trench warfare in the salient as both sides "dug in" around the line.

In military terminology, a salient is an area of territory which projects or bulges into enemy territory. The salient is therefore vulnerable to enemy action on three sides, making the job of holding the salient especially dangerous. The area of the salient on the British side of the line is mostly flat, with few rises or hills. The Germans had the advantage of the higher ground and were able to direct their artillery fire with great accuracy. The struggle to prise the high ground from the Germans was the focus for the 1915 Second Battle of Ypres, which saw the first use of gas and the almost total destruction and evacuation of Ypres, and the 1917 Third Battle of Ypres at Passchendaele.

After the third battle, the Ypres salient was left relatively quiet until the Fourth Battle of Ypres, the Battle of the Lys, when the 1918 German Spring Offensive threatened to overwhelm the entire area. This offensive finally ran out of steam at the moment when the British were considering abandoning the salient. In August 1918, the Fifth Battle of Ypres (part of the Hundred Days Offensive) is the name given to the actions which were designed to eject the German forces out of the salient entirely.

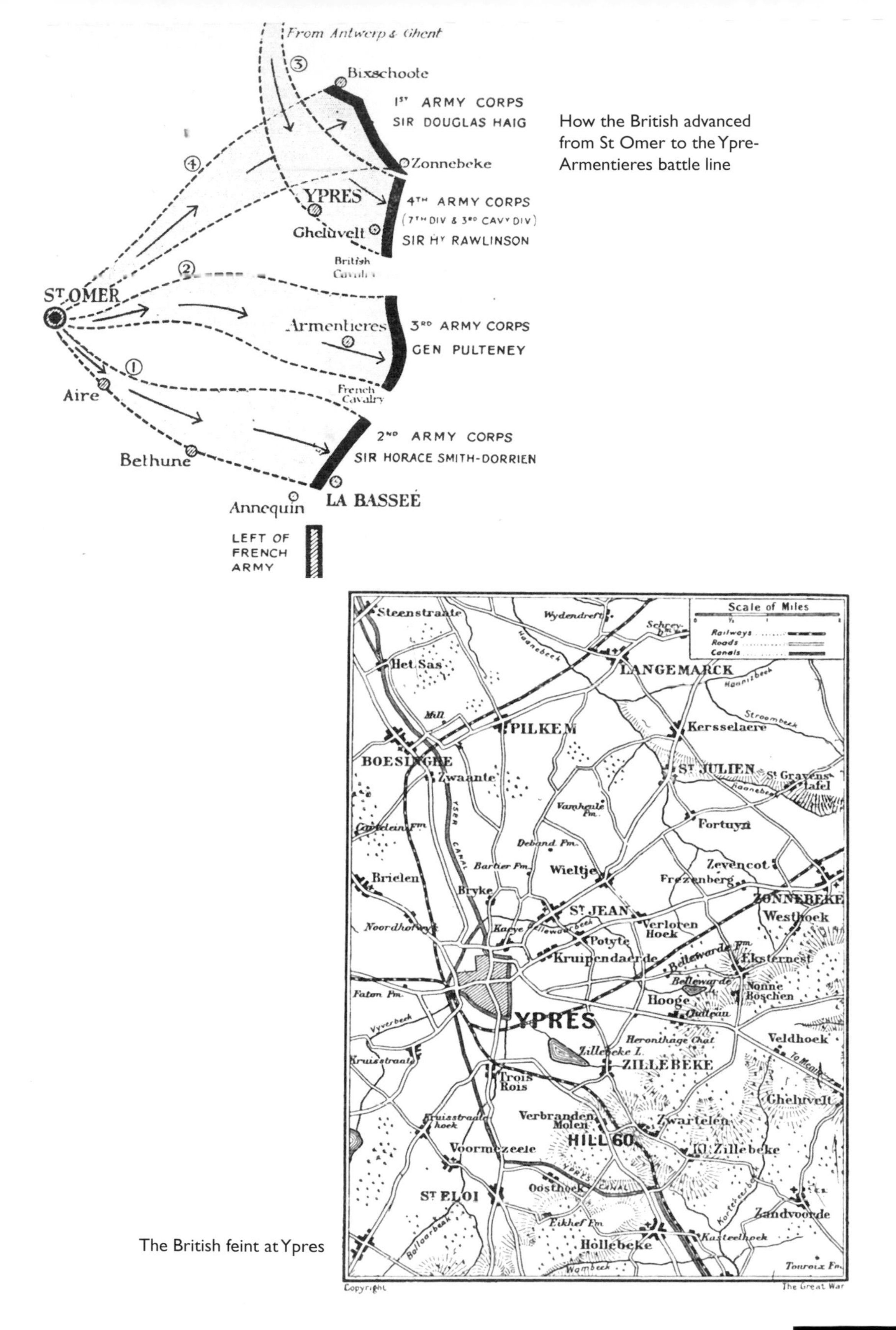

How the British advanced from St Omer to the Ypre-Armentieres battle line

The British feint at Ypres

Opposite: Wounded soldiers charge the Germans - gallant deed of Yorkshire Light Infantry

Fine work of the Lincolns on the Aisne

More nerve racking than the main mast

Wounded first - the most beautiful story of the war

Night attack on the German trenches during the battle of the Aisne

Saving the guns at Siossons - an incident of the fighting on the Aisne

An interlude in the Ypres salient - British officers at 'afternoon tea'.

A gallant Irishman's splendid stand

Women at work that men might fight - Busy scene in one of the munitions workshops in the Summer of 1915

A gallant deed of the West Yorkshires

The first VC ever won by a territorial

Gordon highlanders capturing a German force in the Yser country

'Nosing shells' in one of the factories of Vickers Ltd

How Sergeant O'Leary 'practically captured the enemy's position by himself'

Driving the Germans from their trenches outside burning Ypres

Turning the Germans out of their cover in the woods to the east of Ypres

A British officer gives his life to save that of a wounded enemy

An echo from Neuve Chapelle: A dying officer refuses to leave his regiment

Gallant young Highlander's heroic death near Hooge

Private Lynn's most conspicuous bravery

Drummer Bent's gallantry under fire

Lance Corporal Tombs saves four comrades

Lieutenant Smyth's terrible journey with bombs

A gallant effort to save life under fire

How Lance Corporal Holmes won the V.C.

British transport train near Ypres

Heroism of the 2nd Worcesters at Gheluvelt Chateau near Ypres

The smile of victory

General Sir Horace Lockwood Smith-Dorrien

Germans armed with planks advancing under fire to cross the canals in the Yser district

War behind the curtain of the hills

Men of destiny - the two leaders of the allies in the West

The British under fire - and almost under water

The capture of the German trenches at Neuve Chapelle

Scene at the Blue Cross receiving depot in Northern France

The Northumberland Fusiliers meeting an attack on their first-line trenches at Ypres

King George on the battlefield

King George passing down the battle lines amidst the resounding cheers of the troops

An Anglo-German rifle contest during a lull in the battle

The desperate fighting North of Arras - German attack repulsed

With a British battery at the front - the tense moment when an order arrives by field telephone from the Observation Officer

A sporting chance - British soldiers 'making a dash for it' across an opening in a long sand-bagged communication trench in France

Relief party advancing along 'Regent Street' in Ploegsteert Wood, near Ypres

Watching effect of British gun fire from a sand-bagged ruin near the German lines

Hooded British territorials charging the German trenches at Loos, September 25th 1915

R.A.M.C orderlies giving first-aid to the wounded after a successful advance

Liet.-Colonel Birchall's death while leading the 4th Canadians at Ypres

In British trenches - under shell fire on the battlefield of Neuve Chapelle

With the R.H.A in Flanders - rushing a gun to the firing line

The Manchester Regiment captures the village of Givenchy

Chapter 3

Bruce Bairnsfather Salient warrior

Born to a military family in Murree, British India (now Pakistan), he spent his early life in India, but was brought to England in 1895 to be educated at the United Services College, Westward Ho!, then at Stratford-upon-Avon. Initially intending a military career, he failed entrance exams to Sandhurst and Woolwich Military Academies but joined the Cheshire Regiment.

He resigned in 1907 to become an artist, studying at the John Hassall School of Art. Unsuccessful at first, he worked as an electrical engineer. Working in this capacity for the Old Memorial Theatre, Stratford, brought him into acquaintance with Marie Corelli, who introduced him to Thomas Lipton, a connection that led to commissions to draw advertising sketches for Lipton tea, Player's cigarettes, Keen's Mustard, and Beecham's Pills.

World War I service

"Old Bill", from *Bullets & Billets*: "First Discovered in the Alluvial Deposits of Southern Flanders. Feeds Almost Exclusively on Jam and Water Biscuits. Hobby: Filling Sandbags, on Dark and Rainy Nights".

In 1914 Bruce Bairnsfather joined the Royal Warwickshire Regiment as a second lieutenant and served with a machine gun unit in Flanders until 1915, when he was hospitalised with shellshock and hearing damage sustained during the Second Battle of Ypres. Posted to the 34th Division headquarters on Salisbury Plain, he developed his humorous series for the Bystander focusing on life in the trenches. His work usually featured "Old Bill", a curmudgeonly soldier with trademark walrus moustache and balaclava. The most famous of these illustrations depicts Old Bill with another trooper in a muddy shell hole with shells whizzing all around. The other trooper is grumbling and Bill advises: Well, If you knows of a better 'ole, go to it.

Many of his cartoons from this period were collected in *Fragments From France* (1914) and the autobiographical Bullets & Billets (1916).

Despite the immense popularity with the troops and a massive sales increase for the *Bystander*, initially there were objections to what was viewed as a "vulgar caricature". Nevertheless, their success in raising morale led to Bairnsfather's promotion and receipt of a War Office appointment to draw similar cartoons for other Allied forces.

The Bairnsfather oeuvre is very much the creation of the Ypres salient. In a humorous way it brings home the reality of the fighting in the salient but celebrates the stoicism and determination to succeed which characterised the British army fighting in the most appalling conditions imaginable during 1914 and 1915.

The drawings featured in this section are reproduced with the kind permission of Tonie and Valmai Holt, who have written two books detailing the life and works of Bruce Bairnsfather: *The Best of Fragments from France* and *The Biography of Captain Bruce Bairnsfather*, both published by Pen & Sword Books.

"Well, if you knows a better 'ole go to it!"

The innocent abroad.
OUT SINCE MONS - "Well, what sort of a night 'ave ye 'ad?"
NOVICE (but persistent optimist) - "Oh alright. 'Ad to get out and rest a bit now and again."

"Keep yer 'ead still, or I'll 'ave yer blinkin' ear off!"

"You chuck another sardine at me, my lad, and you'll hear from my solicitors"

Things that matter. Colonel Fitz-Shrapnel receives the following message from "G.H.Q." "Please let us know, as soon as possible, the number of tins of raspberry jam issued to you last Friday."

UP LAST DRAFT - "I suppose you 'as to be careful 'ow you looks over the parapet 'ere" OUT SINCE MONS - "You needn'o worry me lad, the rats are going to be your only trouble"

Directing the way to the front. "Ye know the dead 'orse across the road? Well, keep straight on till ye comes to a perambulator 'longside a Johnson 'ole".

"What time do they feed the sealions, Alf?"

When one would like to start an offensive on one's own. Recipe for feeling like this - bully, biscuits, no coke and leave just cancelled.

The Bystander's Fragments from France

The Bystander's Fragments from France

Above: Owing to dawn breaking sooner than anticipated, that inventive fellow, Private Jones, has a trying time with his latest creation - "The Little Plugstreet" (The Sniper's friend)

Right: "I'm sure they'll hear this damn thing squeaking"

The eternal question. "When the 'ell is it going to be strawberry?"

"Where did that one go to?"

The thirst for reprisals

There is certainly a lot of truth in the Napoleonic maxim, "An army moves on its stomach"

The professional touch. "Chuck us that bag o' bombs, mate; it's under your 'ead".

Situation shortly vacant. In an old established house in France an opening will shortly occur for a young man with good prospects of getting a rise.

"No possible doubt whatever"

Above: Observation. "Ave a squint through these 'ere Bill, you can see one of the ------s eatin' a sausage as clear as anythin'"

Right: Ships that pass in the night. "Where do yer want this put, Sargint?"

The professional instinct again

Left: A Maxim maxim. "Fire should be held till a favourable target presents itself."

Left: "Pop out and get it, Bert"
"Pop out yerself".

Right: "Quick, afore this comes down".

Above: "Give it a good 'ard 'un, Bert, you can generally 'ear 'em fizzin' a bit first if they are a-goin' to explode.

Top right: "Well, Alfred, 'ow are the cakes?"

Right: Having omitted to remove the elastic band prior to descent, Herr Franz von Flopp feels that the trial exhibition of his new parachute is a failure

"They've evidently seen me"

"Stick yer 'at pin into Douglas, Maggie, I've known them things go off before now!"

"There goes our blinkin' parapet again".

Dep. - Paddington 2.15.
Arr. - Home 4

Also available from Pen & Sword Books:

The Best of Fragments from France

ISBN - 978-1-84884-169-7
Paperback
160 pages
£14.99

Bruce Bairnsfather (BB) was the most famous cartoonist of WWI and his soldier characters Old Bill, Bert and Alf, faced with sardonic good humour everything that the Germans, the mud and their officers could throw at them. The cartoons reproduced in this collection were originally drawn for The Bystander, a popular weekly magazine in the Great War. Their effect on the public was so dramatic that Bystander sales soared. The organisation decided to publish the first 43 of his cartoons in an anthology called Fragments from France. Sales quickly reached 250,000 and a second anthology was published. The success of the Fragments magazines was such that edition followed edition and at least eleven editions were published. Leafing through these pages, the reader will soon understand their tremendous popularity and success which have withstood the test of time.

The Biography of Captain Bruce Bairnsfather

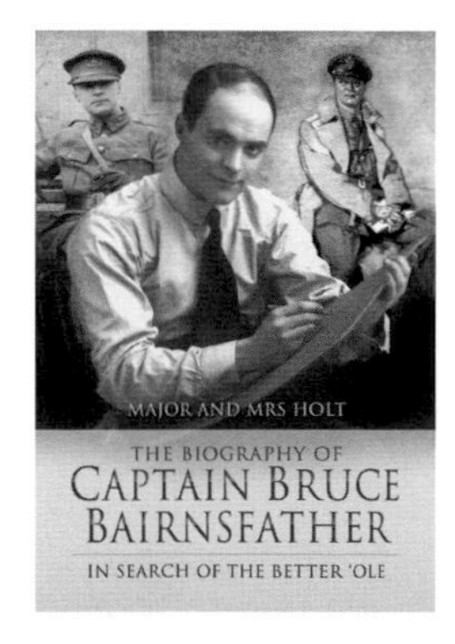

ISBN - 978-1-47382-723-3
Paperback
288 pages
£14.99

Bruce Bairnsfather created one of the best-known cartoon characters of the First World War – 'Old Bill' – and he drew what many consider to be the most enduring cartoon of all time - the 'Better Ole'. During the First World War the contribution of Bairnsfather's work to the morale of the nation, through laughter, is without question. Tonie and Valmai Holt trace his life in fascinating detail. This delightful book reveals a man who was a compelling paradox. Lavishly illustrated with over 150 photographs and drawings, including a useful section setting out the range and values of Bairnsfather memorabilia and collectables.